About the Author

Kathy Tarpley has an adult disabled child; her current passions include writing children's books and wildlife photography.
She lives with her family in Gulf Breeze, Florida.

Thank you for reading my story.
I look forward to reading your review, so please take a moment to post your thoughts on Amazon.

You can also reach the author at freefall32536@yahoo.com.

About the Illustrator

Laura Lembeck-Ejikemeuwa is an artist with over 35 years of experience in Illustration, Product Design and Toy design.
contact at:
lauralembeck365@gmail.com

Exceptionally Special:
I'm Deaf.

My ears don't hear sounds like your ears do...

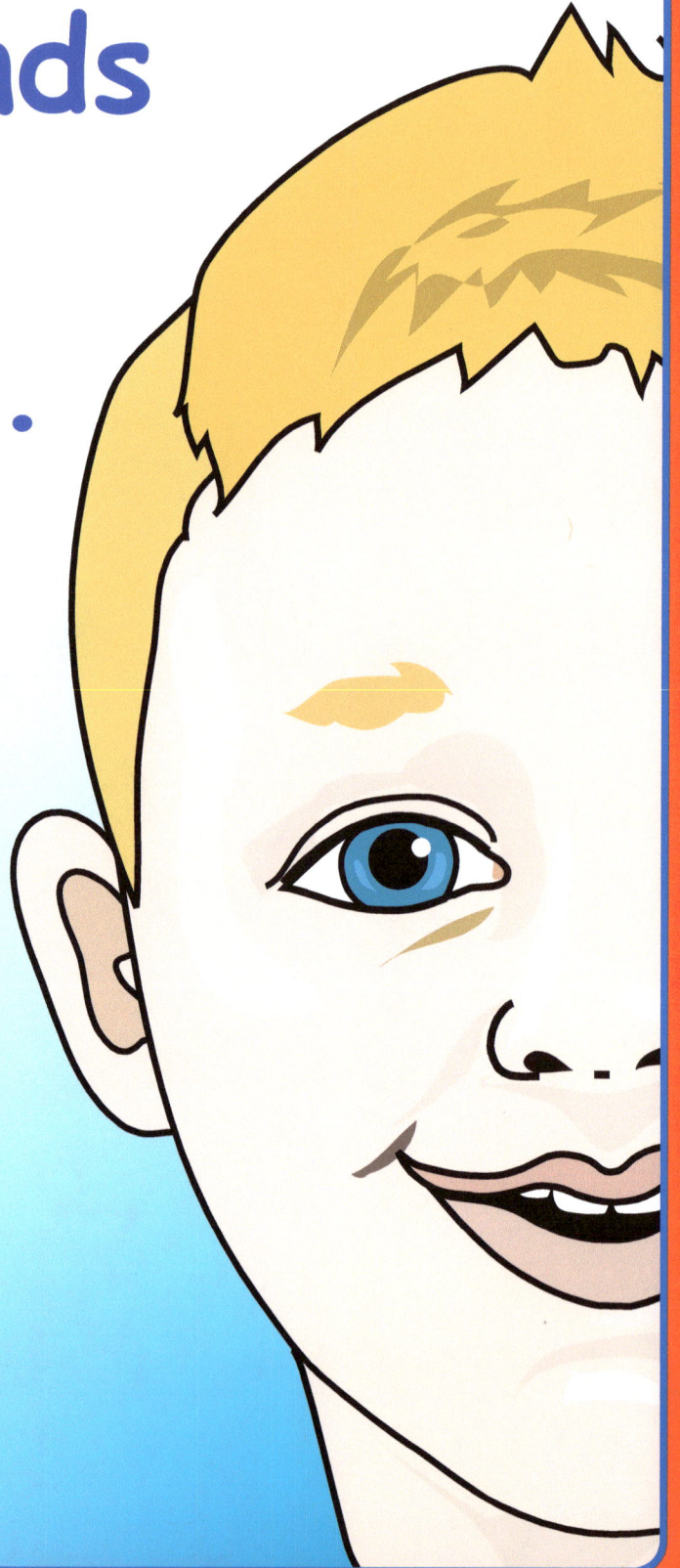

Chirp! Chirp!

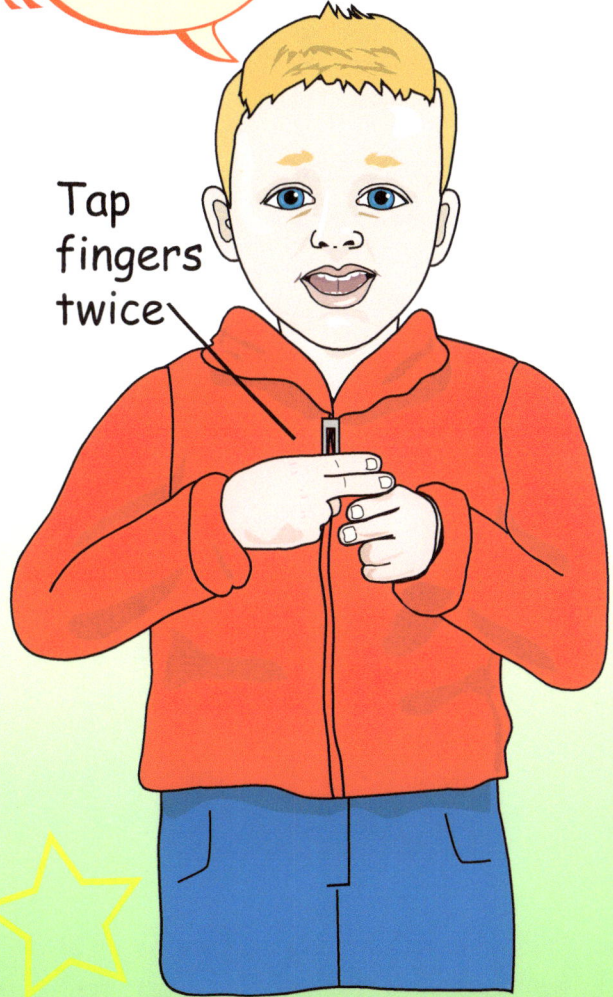

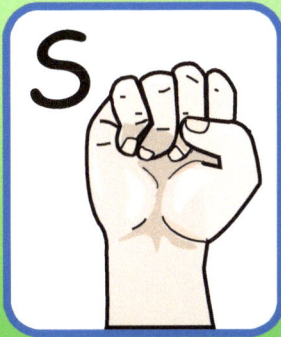

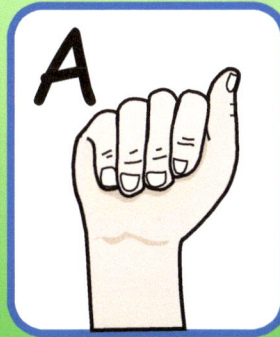

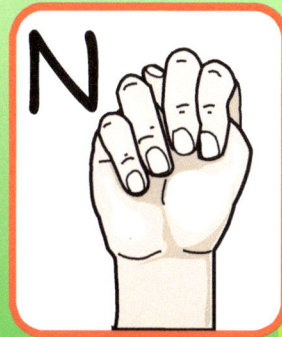

My fingers
can spell letters
like A, B, and C.

I can teach
you how, so you
can speak with me.

A

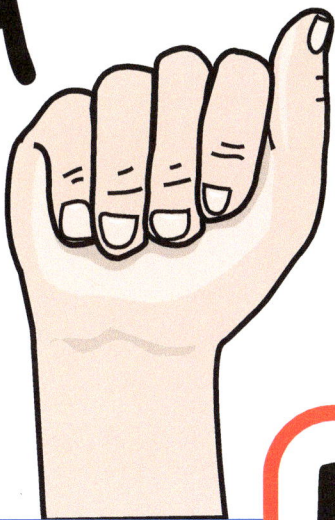

B

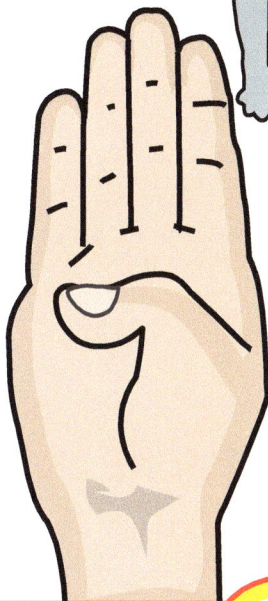

C

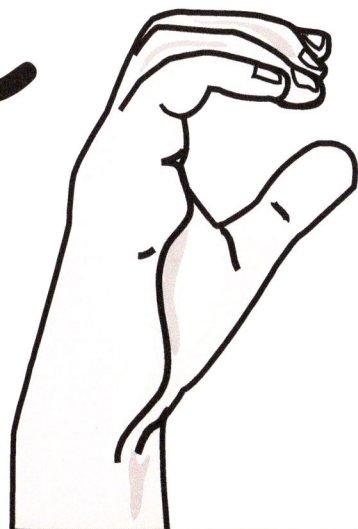

I can teach
you hand signs
to match all your
words, so that
when we talk,
we'll both
be heard,
signs like car
and friend
and tree.

Car

Friend

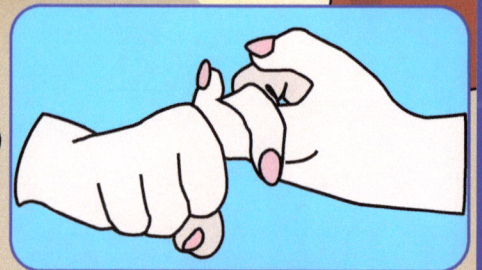

Tree

I'm so excited you want to learn;
So lets get started!
We'll both take turns.

Point to a word, and
I'll teach you the sign.
I'll teach you to talk
with your hands in no time.

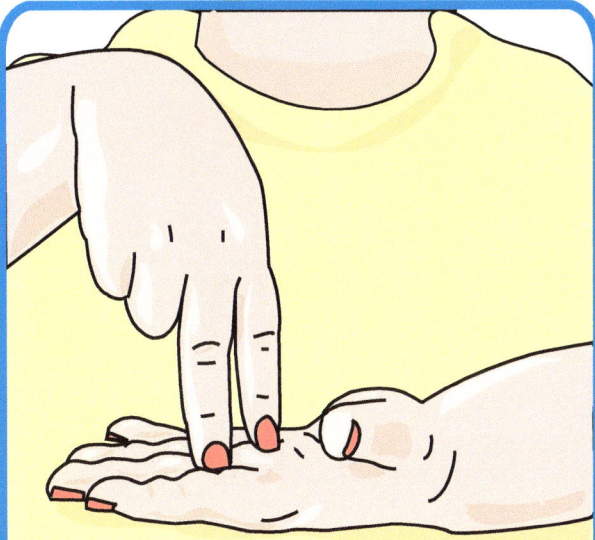

Stand up

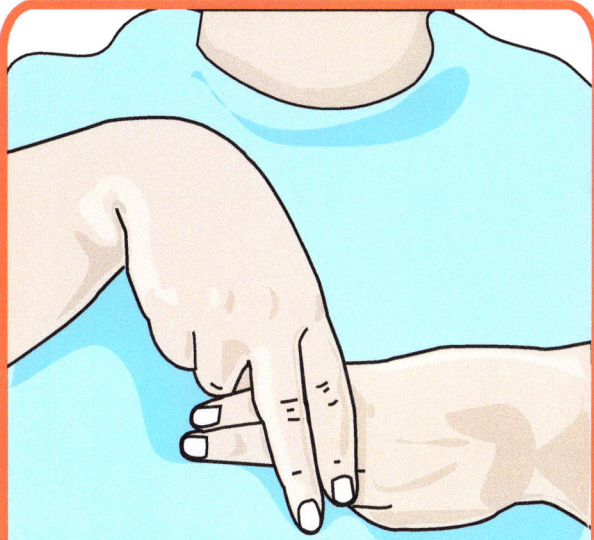

Sit Down

No

Yes

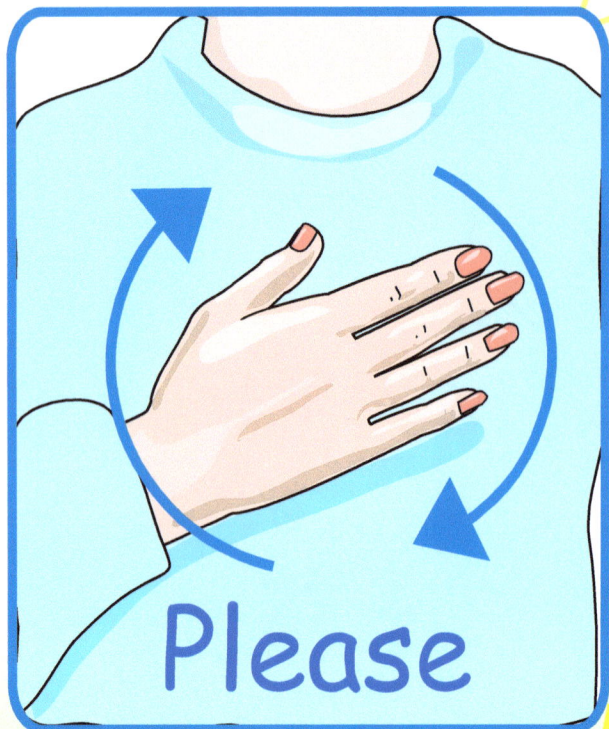

Please

Water

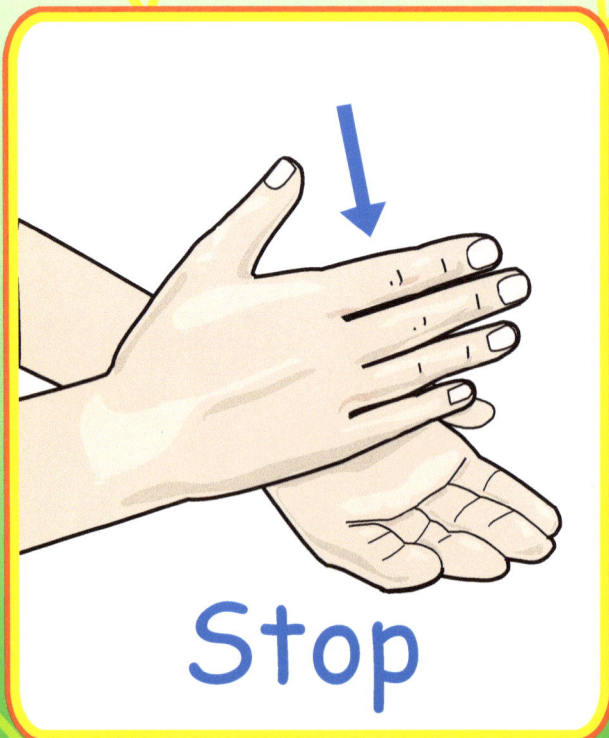

Stop

Help

Sorry

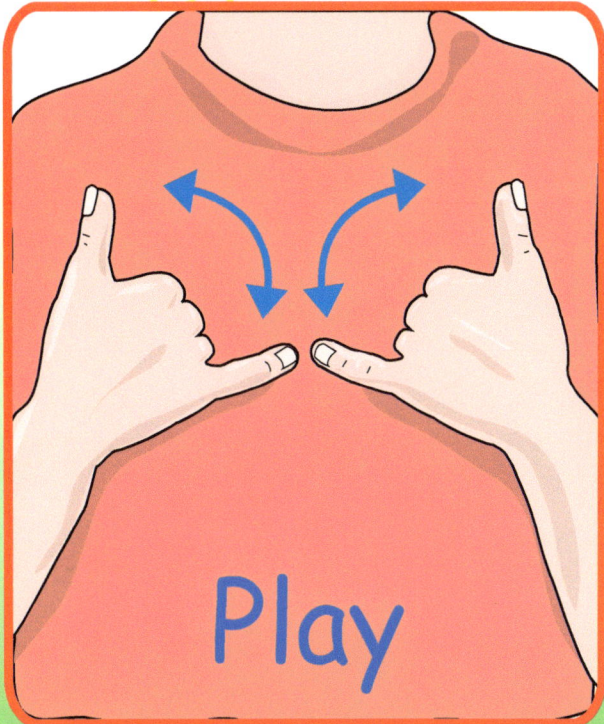

Play

More

Now

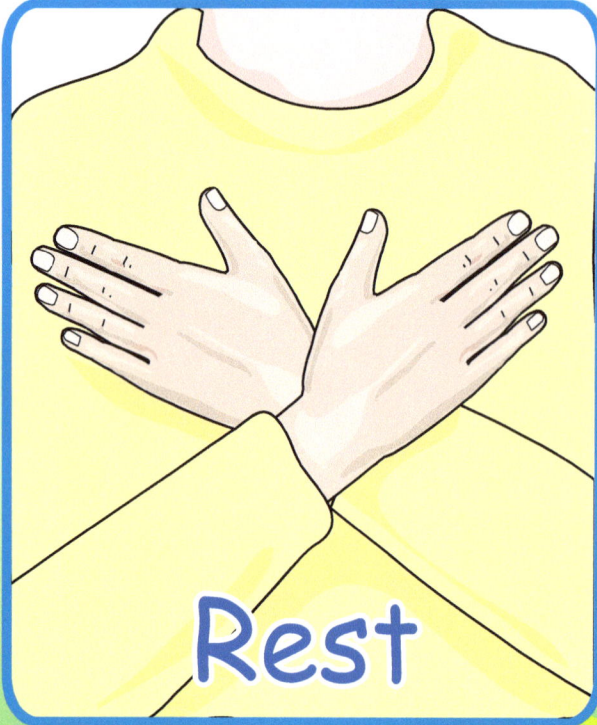

Rest

Bathroom

Mother

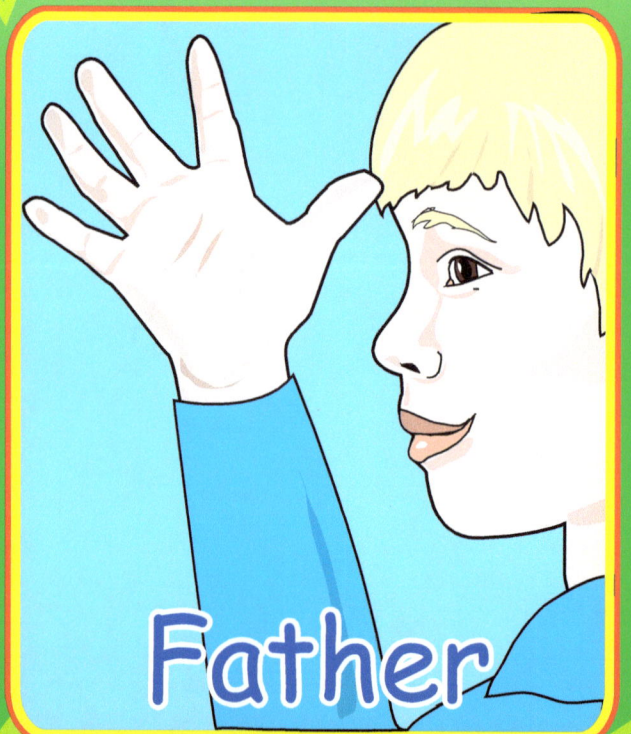

Father

Best sign of all:
I love you.

My ears
are special,
yes that's true,
but I want
to be treated
just like you!

American Sign Language Alphabet

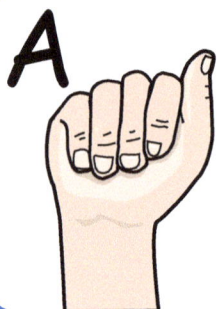

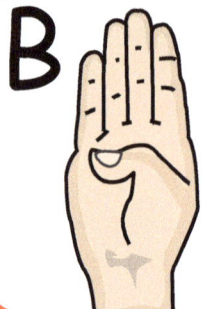

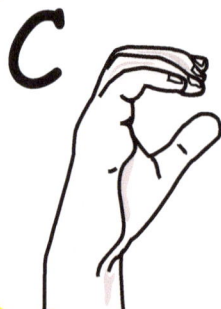

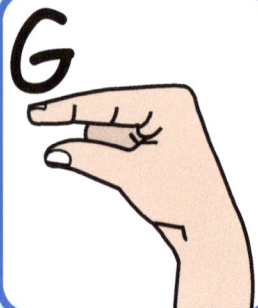

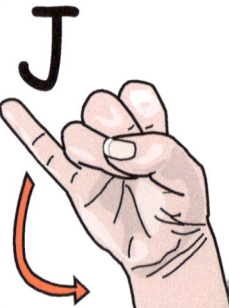

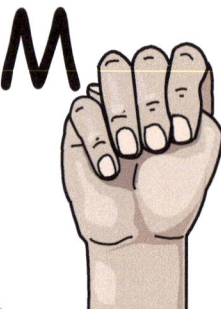

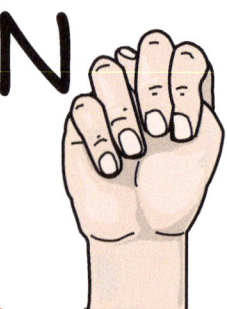

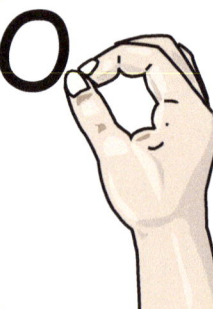

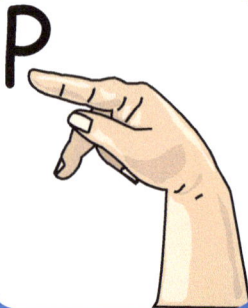

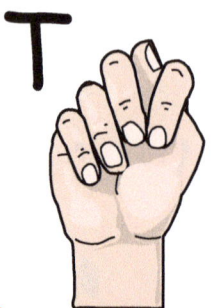

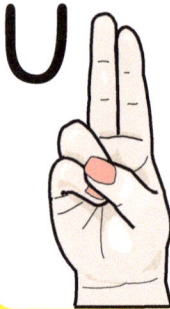

A B C D E

F G H I J

K L M N O

P Q R S T

U V W X Y Z

www.ingramcontent.com/pod-product-compliance
Lightning Source LLC
LaVergne TN
LVHW072116070426
835510LV00002B/89